Transformation:
Pathway to Purpose

Dr Amystique Church

Dedication

To all those in pursuit of purpose, a special nod goes to those who have finally learned to accept their own uniqueness and realize that they do not need anyone's approval.

Be yourself and be free.

Yes, transformation is a journey on the path to process.

Be unapologetically You!

"Success is to be measured not so much by the position that one has reached in life as by the obstacles which he has overcome."
– Booker T. Washington.

Acknowledgment

I am forever grateful to my husband and grown adult children, who have inspired me through the years to pursue my goals and put my passions into action.

A special thank you to my spiritual mother, Katherine "Kitty" Perry, for giving me the opportunity to serve in the community. Mom, Kitty, your teachings have deeply influenced me, and I am committed to continuing to serve the people in the community and stay engaged.

I am also grateful to Naomie Y. Church for her contributions (research, graphics design, chapter titles, and themes).

Thank you, Autumn Lewis, Shasta Holt, Ellen Dunn, Victoria Harris, and Aubrianna Brinkley; thank you for your insight, answering questions, and being a part of this journey.

About the Author

Amystique is a wife, mother, and grandmother (Nana/Mema) and lives in Delaware with her husband, Kirby Sr.

She has a passion for serving and making a difference in others' lives because she understands first-hand what it means to go from tragedy to triumph, from need to plenty, from termination/loss to success/gain.

Contents

Personal Growth

Personal growth involves aligning your emotions, mental health, and overall harmony with life. It requires raw honesty and a willingness to face truths about oneself.

Think of your life as a vibrant symphony composed of experiences, relationships, and aspirations. Personal growth allows you to shape the melody of this symphony actively, ensuring the notes resonate with your core values and harmonize into a beautiful composition. Even the renowned psychologist Abraham Maslow, when proposing a hierarchy of needs, placed self-actualization (the need for personal growth and fulfillment) at the very pinnacle.[1] Personal growth isn't about external validation or achieving societal expectations; it's about aligning your life with your authentic self and forging a path toward a meaningful existence. It involves six stages, each a crucial steppingstone towards a more fulfilling life:

1. Unknowing

This is the starting point, often shrouded in a comfortable ignorance. The stage of unknowing is where you might be blissfully unaware of areas needing improvement. Perhaps you're stuck in a routine, feeling a vague sense of discontent but unable to pinpoint the source.

This stage isn't inherently negative; it's simply the starting point, the fertile ground from which growth can spring.

---

[1] McLeod, S. A. (2018, May 21). Maslow's hierarchy of needs. Retrieved from https://www.simplypsychology.org/maslow.html

2.Awareness

A chance encounter with a mentor, a thought-provoking book, or even a seemingly mundane event can spark the flame of awareness. Suddenly, you see your life through a new lens, realizing that your current path might not be leading to fulfillment. This "aha" moment can be exhilarating yet unsettling. The initial excitement of awareness can be followed by resistance.

3.Acceptance

The stage of acceptance can be the most challenging. A wave of resistance can replace the initial excitement of awareness. You might grapple with the reality of your limitations, the fear of change, or the uncertainty of the unknown. But it is a crucial moment.

Denial might feel comfortable in the short term, but it hinders growth. Acceptance, however difficult, allows you to acknowledge the need for change and pave the way for progress.

4.Responsibility

This stage marks a turning point. You move from passively acknowledging the need for change to actively taking ownership of your growth journey. You are the architect, now committed to designing the blueprint for your transformation. Here, the analogy of Stephen Covey's "Circle of Influence" from his book "The 7 Habits of Highly Effective People" becomes particularly relevant.[2] Imagine yourself standing in the center of two

---

[2] https://dplearningzone.the-dp.co.uk/wp-content/uploads/sites/2/2015/06/Covey.pdf

concentric circles. The inner circle represents your **Circle of Influence**. This circle encompasses all the aspects of your life that you have direct control over – your thoughts, beliefs, emotions, actions, and behaviors. It's your sphere of influence, the space where you can make deliberate choices and initiate change.

The outer circle represents your **Circle of Concern**. This circle encompasses everything that affects you, including external factors like the weather, economic conditions, the actions of others, and world events. While you can't directly control these external forces, you can control how you respond to them. Taking responsibility empowers you to become the driving force behind your own evolution.

5. Application

This is where the rubber meets the road. You translate your newfound awareness and commitment into concrete actions. This might involve enrolling in a course to develop a new skill, seeking therapy to address emotional blocks, or simply incorporating mindfulness practices into your daily routine. These actions become the tools you wield to sculpt your growth, shaping yourself into the best version of who you can be.

6. Purpose

Through sustained effort and self-reflection, you discover the "why" behind your growth journey. Your brand-new awareness fuels a sense of purpose, guiding your actions and decisions. Viktor Frankl, the Holocaust survivor and author of "Man's Search for Meaning," reminds us, "*It's not about finding the meaning of life, but rather about creating it.*" Your purpose might evolve over time, but its essence lies in contributing something meaningful to the world and aligning your actions with your core values.

Professional Growth

Professional growth is a journey of exploration, strategy, and continuous advancement. It's not simply about climbing the corporate ladder or earning a bigger paycheck. True professional growth is about finding fulfillment, purpose, and a sense of deep satisfaction in your job. It's about waking up each day excited to go to work, feeling challenged and appreciated, and knowing that your work makes a difference.

Let me ask you: are you satisfied with your career? Many dedicate years to their careers, pouring their energy and talents into their professional pursuits. But what happens when the initial spark fades? When the daily grind replaces excitement, and dissatisfaction creeps in? Professional growth becomes the antidote to this stagnation. It allows you to re-evaluate your career path, identify areas for improvement, and ultimately, design a work life that aligns with your values and aspirations. Think of your career as a dynamic skillset, each skill a valuable commodity you bring to the marketplace. Through professional growth, you actively curate this skillset, adding new offerings and ensuring you remain a valuable asset in today's ever-changing workplace. Peter Drucker emphasized the importance of continuous learning in his book "The Practice of Management," arguing that individuals and organizations must constantly adapt and learn to remain competitive.[3] In the ultimate end, it is about

---

[3] https://www.econstor.eu/bitstream/10419/90303/1/773159398.pdf

being happy, filled with joy, and content. No amount of money or high-status title can substitute for these essential feelings.

The path to attaining professional growth is an ongoing process, not a one-time event. Take the time to reflect on your career and consider these steps to ensure that your professional path aligns with your personal fulfillment:

1. Set Goals

Preparation is the foundation of a successful career. Setting clear, achievable goals is essential for guiding your professional trajectory. Begin by contemplating where you envision yourself in the future – in five years, ten years, or even further down the road. What are your aspirations, and what steps do you need to take to achieve them?

Start by setting **SMART goals** – Specific, Measurable, Achievable, Relevant, and Time-bound. Ask yourself: *What skills do I want to develop to advance in my field? What experiences am I seeking to broaden my professional knowledge? What does a healthy work-life balance look like for me?* For instance, if your aim is to advance to a managerial position, a specific goal could be obtaining leadership training or completing a relevant certification within a set timeframe. Break these overarching goals into smaller, actionable steps to ensure steady progress. By clearly defining your goals, you establish a roadmap that guides your journey through the professional marketplace.

2. Document Your Development

Just as a skilled artist study their own techniques to refine their craft, you need to understand your strengths and weaknesses to steer professional growth effectively. Self-reflection is key.

Documenting your development allows you to track your progress, recognize your achievements, and identify areas for improvement. Take the time to reflect on your career journey thus far. What milestones have you reached? What challenges have you overcome?

Consider taking personality assessments, soliciting feedback from trusted colleagues, and keeping a career journal to track your progress. This self-awareness empowers you to identify areas for improvement and capitalize on your existing skills.

3. Assess Skills and Knowledge Gaps

Exploration involves critically evaluating your current skills and knowledge in relation to your career aspirations. The bustling marketplace offers diverse stalls, some familiar, others presenting exciting new discoveries.

Research industry trends, explore emerging skillsets within your field, and identify any gaps between your current skillset and your aspirations. This might involve attending industry conferences, networking with professionals in your desired career path, or reading relevant books and articles.

Engage in continuous learning and skill development to remain relevant in a rapidly evolving professional landscape. Explore opportunities for further education, training programs, or hands-on experiences that can enhance your capabilities. Embrace challenges and seek out projects that push you outside your comfort zone, allowing you to expand your skill set and grow as a professional.

4. Create an Action Plan for Success

This final stage is about translating your brand-new awareness and goals into concrete action. Develop a professional development plan that outlines specific steps you'll take to bridge skill gaps, expand your knowledge base, and achieve your career goals.

Break down your goals into manageable tasks and set deadlines for each. There will be moments of doubt and setbacks along the way. The key is to embrace these challenges, learn from them, and maintain a growth mindset. Stay flexible and open to adapting your plan as needed in response to changing circumstances or opportunities that may arise. Let curiosity be your guide, celebrate your progress, and never stop exploring the limitless possibilities that lie within your professional path.

Remember, true professional success is measured not by titles or monetary rewards but by the joy, contentment, and happiness you experience in your work.

Take ownership of your career path, remain open to growth and learning opportunities, and strive to create a fulfilling and meaningful professional life.

Spiritual Growth

In the pursuit of spiritual growth, you must be willing to commence your journey of self-discovery and connection with a higher power. Spiritual enrichment is an ongoing process of deepening our understanding of ourselves and our connection to the divine. It's not about subscribing to a specific religion or dogma; it's about fostering a deeper connection to a source of meaning, purpose, and a sense of belonging within the universe.

Unlike other forms of growth, spiritual growth cannot be achieved once and for all; rather, it is a continuous process that evolves and unfolds over time.

Many people navigate life on autopilot, their days filled with routines and responsibilities. Spiritual growth disrupts this autopilot mode, prompting you to explore the deeper questions of existence and your place within it. I believe that even in the darkest of circumstances, the human spirit can find meaning and purpose. Spiritual growth allows you to cultivate this inner strength, fostering a sense of peace, connection, and a deeper appreciation for the world around you.

Think of your spirit as a radiant light meant to shine brightly within the cosmos. Spiritual growth allows you to nourish this light, removing any obstructions that might dim its brilliance. Wayne Dyer emphasizes the importance of self-love and acceptance and asserts that true spiritual growth begins with loving ourselves unconditionally, allowing our inner light to shine forth more powerfully.[4] Just as a magnificent tree requires consistent nourishment to thrive, so too does your spirit. To cultivate spiritual growth, engaging in daily practices that foster a deeper connection with God and nourish the soul is essential. These practices serve as pillars of spiritual enrichment, guiding us on our journey toward greater spiritual maturity.

---

[4] https://www.drwaynedyer.com/blog/divine-love-meet-your-true-self/

One of the foundational practices for spiritual growth is the daily reading of sacred texts such as the Bible or other spiritual books. These texts contain timeless wisdom and insights that can inspire and guide us on our spiritual journey. Set aside time each day to immerse yourself in these sacred writings, reflecting on their meaning and relevance to your life.

Prayer and meditation are powerful tools for deepening our connection with God and quieting the mind. Through prayer, we communicate with the divine, expressing our gratitude, seeking guidance, and offering praise. Meditation, on the other hand, allows us to quiet the noise of the outside world and attune ourselves to the presence of God within. Make time each day for prayer and meditation, creating a sacred space where you can commune with the divine and nurture your soul.

Another essential aspect of spiritual growth is discovering your calling and purpose in life. What are your interests, passions, and talents? What brings you joy and fulfillment? Reflect on these questions and seek guidance from God to uncover your unique purpose. Your calling may be found in serving others, pursuing creative endeavors, or simply being present in the world's beauty and wonder. Embrace your calling with openness and humility, trusting that God has a plan for your life. Finally, fellowship with like-minded individuals who share your desire for spiritual growth is essential for nurturing your soul. Surround yourself with a community of faith where you can find support, encouragement, and accountability on your spiritual journey. Participate in worship services, small group discussions, or spiritual retreats where you can connect with others who are also seeking to deepen their relationship with

God. Together, you can inspire one another, share insights, and walk the path of spiritual growth hand in hand.

Spiritual growth is not about self-isolation; it's about fostering meaningful connections and contributing to something larger than yourself. Volunteer your time or skills to a cause you care about. Simple acts of kindness can have a reflective impact on yourself and those around you. Helping others connects you to the world in a powerful way and strengthens your sense of purpose. Embrace the journey with an open heart and a spirit of curiosity, knowing that God is with you every step of the way.

The Paradox of Transformation

Transformation isn't a singular, controlled event; it's a dynamic dance between forces beyond our control and those we can actively influence.

We exist within a swirling vortex of external forces — societal expectations, unexpected events, and the natural flow of life. These forces can be the catalyst for change, pushing us out of our comfort zones and propelling us towards transformation.

However, we aren't simply passive bystanders in all this. We possess the agency to pilot the external forces by cultivating self-awareness and taking action. This is where self-evaluation becomes the critical tool for navigating the transformation process. By dissecting our thoughts, emotions, and experiences, we gain insights into our values, desires, and areas for growth. This self-evaluation allows us to identify patterns, understand our reactions to external stimuli, and ultimately, make conscious choices that shape the direction of our transformation. But this journey of transformation is rarely a linear path with a clear destination. The "full picture" you seek might remain obscured by the swirling forces of change. It's easy to become fixated on the "ultimate purpose" and lose sight of the present moment. This lack of clarity can be unsettling, triggering anxiety and a desperate need for control. Instead, shift your focus to the tasks and experiences right in front of you. By diligently completing today's tasks and staying present on the current path, you pave the way for a future that unfolds organically.

There will also be moments of regression, where you find yourself revisiting old patterns or questioning your path. This back-and-forth movement is a natural part of the process. Don't be discouraged by these setbacks; see them as opportunities for deeper reflection and course correction. In moments of doubt and despair, holding onto hope and faith is essential. Ephesians 1:18 reminds us that by having our "eyes of the heart flooded with light," we gain insights into the purpose behind our journey. This "light" represents self-awareness, guiding us towards actions that align with our deepest values and calling. The passage reminds us that transformation isn't simply a personal quest; it's about connecting to something larger than ourselves. Just as the volcanic eruption enriches the surrounding soil, our transformation allows us to contribute positively to the world around us.

The Necessity of Transformation in a Demanding World

Life's demands can be relentless, with a constant barrage of challenges and responsibilities that require a certain level of adaptability and resilience. Here's where transformation becomes crucial. It equips you with the tools to manage negative emotions, foster positive thinking, and, ultimately, cultivate the peace and contentment necessary to enjoy the journey.

Nina Amir identifies the ten compelling reasons to embark on your personal growth journey.[5] As you ponder these reasons, take a moment for reflection:

1. **To Get Unstuck:** Life can throw curveballs, leaving you feeling stagnant and unsure of your next move. Personal growth empowers you to break free from these limitations, identify new possibilities, and move forward with renewed purpose.

2. **To Overcome Fear:** Fear can be a paralyzing force, hindering your progress. Through personal growth, you develop the tools to confront your fears, build confidence, and embrace challenges with courage and determination.

3. **To Feel More Confident:** Confidence is like fertile soil, nourishing your sense of self-worth and empowering you to take risks, pursue your dreams, and deal with life's complexities with greater ease. Personal growth allows you to cultivate this confidence, building a foundation for a fulfilling and successful life.

4. **To Experience More Joy:** Life isn't meant to be lived in perpetual stress and anxiety. Personal growth helps you develop a positive outlook, appreciate life's simple pleasures, and cultivate a sense of joy that enriches your daily existence.

---

[5] https://ninaamir.com/reasons-focus-personal-growth/

5. **To Experience More Love:** Love, in all its forms, is essential for a meaningful and fulfilling life. Personal growth fosters self-love, allowing you to show up authentically in your relationships and build stronger, more meaningful connections with others.

6. **To Improve Your Health:** The mind and body are deeply interconnected. Personal growth practices that cultivate stress management, positive self-talk, and healthy habits contribute significantly to improved physical and emotional well-being.

7. **To Increase Your Income:** While personal growth isn't solely about financial gain, it can positively impact your earning potential. By developing new skills, enhancing your communication skills, and building confidence, you position yourself for advancement or create opportunities to pursue lucrative career paths.

8. **To Have Better Relationships:** Effective communication, empathy, and healthy boundaries are essential for strong relationships. Personal growth fosters these qualities, allowing you to build more fulfilling connections with family, friends, and colleagues.

9. **To Achieve More Success:** Success is a subjective concept, but personal growth equips you with the tools to define your own version of success and pursue it with focus, perseverance, and a positive attitude.

10. **To Achieve Your Dreams:** Deep within us all lie dreams waiting to be realized. Personal growth empowers you to

identify these dreams, develop a roadmap to achieve them, and overcome obstacles in your way.

The concept of self-care has often been misconstrued as a fleeting indulgence – a massage, a shopping spree, a fleeting moment of escape. However, true self-care, the foundation of "self-full self-care," is a deliberate, daily practice. It's about holistically nurturing your emotional, mental, spiritual, and physical well-being.

Remember, this transformation begins from within. As you prioritize your well-being, your life will blossom in unexpected ways. Challenges are inevitable, but just as day follows night, breakthroughs follow trials. The process starts with self-care, then transforms into action, positive self-talk, firm faith, and, ultimately, transformative change. Don't be discouraged by the seemingly insurmountable staircase ahead. Take the first step, embrace the journey, and witness the extraordinary unfold before you. As Martin Luther King Jr. stated, *"You don't have to see the whole staircase. Just take the first step."*

Chapter 2: Step into the New

Imagine yourself standing at the precipice of a mountain peak. The wind whispers secrets through your hair, carrying the scent of wildflowers and pine. Below, a hidden path snakes its way through a valley painted in vibrant hues, beckoning you toward the unknown.

This, my friend, is the threshold of your transformation – a portal to a version of yourself brimming with potential, waiting to be discovered. It's a call that has echoed throughout history, a yearning knitted into the very fabric of our humanity.

From the philosophical musings of ancient Greeks to the cutting-edge research of modern psychology, the human desire for self-discovery and fulfillment resonates across time and culture.

Aristotle, a titan of ancient philosophy, declared happiness (or "**eudaimonia**" in Greek) as the ultimate human goal, not just a fleeting feeling of pleasure.[6] This eudaimonia translates more accurately to "flourishing" – a state of well-being that encompasses fleeting joy and a deep sense of purpose and living authentically.

Eastern philosophies also echo this sentiment, where the teachings of the Buddha emphasize escaping suffering and achieving a state of lasting happiness, a state synonymous with liberation. Even the Declaration of Independence of the United States enshrines the "pursuit of happiness" as a fundamental

---

[6] Melchert, N. (2002). Aristotle: The reality of the world. The good life. *The great conversation: A historical introduction to philosophy, 4*, 186-198

right, recognizing its centrality to a meaningful life. The Dalai Lama, a beacon of wisdom and compassion, underscores the universal desire to overcome suffering and find happiness, a desire he believes everyone has the right to fulfill.

The recent explosion of positive psychology as a scientific field further validates this enduring human quest. Founded less than two decades ago by pioneers like Martin Seligman, positive psychology has taken the world by storm. This field isn't about chasing fleeting highs; it's about cultivating the conditions for lasting well-being, for a life that is not just happy but deeply fulfilling.[7]

The PERMA Model

Building on the wisdom of Aristotle, Seligman acknowledges the importance of positive emotions but emphasizes that happiness is a multifaceted experience. He proposes PERMA, an acronym capturing the key elements of well-being: **Positive emotions, Engagement, Relationships, Meaning, and Achievement**. Think of PERMA as your compass, guiding you towards a life filled with purpose and fulfillment.

Consider Positive emotions – the moments of joy, satisfaction, and contentment that color our lives. But happiness is not just about feeling good; it's also about feeling engaged and fully absorbed in activities that challenge and reward us. Relationships are the cornerstone of human connection, providing us with a sense of belonging, love, and support.

---

[7] Seligman, M. (2011). *Flourish: A visionary new understanding of happiness and well-being*. New York, NY: Simon and Schuster

Meaning that elusive yet potent force propels us forward. The sense of purpose drives us to contribute something valuable to the world. And finally, Achievement, the satisfaction of setting goals and accomplishing them, builds our confidence and propels us further along our path.

The Layers of You

Stepping into the new and truly understanding yourself is not a single step; it's a transformative journey. Imagine yourself as an onion, with layers that gradually reveal your core. This journey of self-discovery requires peeling back those layers to identify what hinders your transformation.

We've all had those moments of self-sabotage, those instances where we look back at past situations and cringe, wondering, *"Why did I do that?"*. Holding onto regrets and the *should have, would have* mentality is like dragging an anchor – it weighs you down and prevents you from moving forward. These regrets and limiting beliefs become shadows that dim our light and hold us back from reaching our full potential.

We must liberate ourselves from the shackles of regret to step into the new. This doesn't mean forgetting the past; it means acknowledging our mistakes, learning from them, and letting go of the crippling grip of self-criticism. Embrace the powerful mantra: **Forgive, Forget, Move On, and Succeed**. Forgiveness extends not just to others but also to yourself. Forgive yourself for past missteps, learn from them, and release yourself from the prison of self-doubt. Imagine a caterpillar, a humble creature inching across a leaf. One day, a profound shift begins. It spins a silk cocoon, a temporary tomb, and undergoes a breathtaking transformation. Inside, it dissolves, its very being rearranging into something entirely new. When it emerges, it's no longer a crawling caterpillar but a magnificent butterfly capable of soaring through vibrant skies.

This is a metaphor for your own transformation. Like the caterpillar, you are also destined for a metamorphosis. Like a vast ecosystem, life presents opportunities for constant change, an ascent from one form to another. Like animals moving through their life cycles, we also evolve, shedding old skins and embracing the new.

The "new" can initially feel like uncharted territory, a wilderness shrouded in uncertainty. It can trigger a primal fear of the unknown. Stepping into new spaces, meeting unfamiliar faces, and encountering novel experiences can be unsettling.

However, remember – the caterpillar likely didn't relish the confines of its cocoon, yet that transformation birthed its ability to fly.

Personal change necessitates venturing beyond the familiar. It requires us to act, think, and be in entirely new ways. Transformation isn't a destination; it's a constant process – a persistent pursuit of a better, more fulfilled you.

Think of it as a journey towards a magnificent mountain peak. The path may be arduous, but the view from the summit is unparalleled.

So, how do we bridge the gap between the familiar and the frighteningly new? The answer lies in **innovation** – the act of embracing fresh ideas and venturing down untrodden paths. Innovation is the lifeblood of progress. Every major advancement in human history – from harnessing the power of electricity to the digital revolution – stemmed from minds daring to break free from the shackles of convention.

Imagine trying to reach the summit of that mountain by clinging to the same rock face repeatedly, expecting a different outcome. Innovation is the act of finding a new route, a bolder approach. Without embracing the new, achieving genuine transformation remains a distant dream.

Look around you. The very world we inhabit is a testament to the power of innovation. The shift from the Industrial Revolution, where we harnessed the power of water and steam, to the digital age, filled with electronics and automation, all happened because people dared to try something new.

Your transformation mirrors this larger narrative of progress. As you shift, you, too, are creating a new version of yourself, one imbued with innovation and the courage to embrace the unknown.

The Butterfly Emerges

Ah, the golden days of childhood, simpler times when passing primary school was perhaps the pinnacle of achievement, a surefire way to earn your parent's beaming approval. Success back then was a straightforward equation – stellar grades on tests and meticulous completion of homework assignments.

The formula was clear: study diligently, regurgitate the information on tests, and voila – academic victory. But what if you stumbled on that first test, and the grade fell short of your (or perhaps your parent's) expectations? Hypothetically speaking, imagine your wise teacher, recognizing your potential, offers a lifeline – a chance to retake the test, armed with the additional weapon of an hour of personalized tutoring. This tutoring session represents a new approach, a concentrated method of study designed to propel you toward success. It's a turning point, a crossroads.

Would you cling stubbornly to your old study habits, the ones that yielded less-than-stellar results? Or would you embrace innovation, grasping at this novel approach like a lifeline?

The truth is, the "old" you cannot navigate the uncharted territories that lie ahead. New experiences, new places – they demand a new version of you, one forged in the fires of audacity and a willingness to shed the comfort of the familiar. This new you must step out of the well-worn grooves of your comfort zone and into the exhilarating yet daunting realm of boldness.

Boldness is the key that unlocks the treasure chest of your hidden potential. It fuels the relentless pursuit of your dreams, pushing you towards transformation with unbendable determination.

"If you want change, YOU must change. If you change, everything will change for you. When you get better, everything will get better for you."

- Jim Rohn.

Stepping out of your comfort zone is, by definition, uncomfortable. That unsettling feeling whispers doubts in your ear, urging you to retreat to the familiar. But don't be fooled by this discomfort; it's not a sign that you've strayed from the path. Instead, view it as a potent catalyst, a spark that ignites your journey of growth. Researchers Kaitlin Woolley and Ayelet Fishbach, through a series of five studies involving over 2,000 participants, explored the power of discomfort as a motivator for personal growth. The study revealed that by employing "cognitive reappraisal," the act of assigning a new meaning to discomfort, participants experienced a heightened sense of achievement and personal expression. This strategy goes beyond merely tolerating discomfort; it encourages you to seek it out actively.

The risk you take to transform yourself is not a reckless leap into the void; it's a calculated chance to hone new skills and build resilience. Discomfort, once a barrier, becomes a beacon, guiding you toward a future brimming with potential. It's no longer a stopping point but a source of motivation, driving you forward on your transformative journey.

Remember, the magnificent butterfly that graces the skies wasn't always so. It emerged from a cocoon, a place of discomfort and transformation.

So, embrace the discomfort, for within it lies the key to unlocking the extraordinary version of yourself waiting to be discovered.

Fuel for Your Transformation

The metamorphosis you're undertaking, this journey towards a brand-new you, requires a potent fuel to keep you moving forward – **firm motivation**. This motivation stems from an intrinsic desire to learn and grow, a yearning for knowledge and self-improvement. But motivation is just one piece of the

puzzle. Here's where another crucial element enters the scene –
your **mindset**. Picture your mindset as the invisible architect
shaping your life's blueprint. It encompasses your beliefs,
assumptions, and expectations about yourself, your capabilities,
and the world around you. Understanding, adapting, and
ultimately shifting your mindset becomes paramount when
navigating the challenges and discomforts that inevitably arise on
the path to transformation.

This goes far beyond simply maintaining a *can-do* attitude.
It's about cultivating a deep-seated belief that you will reach your
desired destination. It's about believing in the expectations you
set for yourself and placing them into the fabric of your thoughts
and actions. This is the essence of "**walking the talk**" – aligning
your internal narrative with your outward behavior.

Remember our earlier discussion about reframing discomfort
as a catalyst for growth? The ability to adapt your mindset plays
a pivotal role in this process. By adjusting your perspective on
discomfort, you can dismantle any limiting beliefs that might hold
you back.

A maladaptive or fixed mindset acts as a barrier to growth.
It's the belief that your intelligence, skills, and talents are fixed
entities, unchangeable throughout your life.

For example, if you struggle with leadership in group settings,
a fixed mindset might convince you that you're not a leader,
forever doomed to remain on the sidelines. This mindset fosters
a deep aversion to opportunities that stretch your comfort zone.
Staying stagnant in your comfort zone might feel safe, but it also
means missing out on experiences that could propel you forward.

With a fixed mindset, taking chances feels akin to trying to change the color of your hair – an impossible feat. This lack of motivation and ambition cripples your ability to transform and reach your full potential.

The growth mindset, on the other hand, is a beacon of hope on your journey. It signifies an openness to challenges and a willingness to learn from every positive and negative experience. Setbacks are no longer viewed as crippling failures but as stepping stones on the path to mastery. Challenges become exciting obstacles to overcome, opportunities to test your new skills and emerge stronger.

The growth mindset fosters resilience and persistence, empowering you to push through moments of anxiety and disappointment. Individuals with a growth mindset are more likely to invest the effort required to achieve their goals, experiencing less stress and self-doubt along the way.

Conversely, a fixed mindset, often referred to as an **"entity theory of personality,"** leads to the opposite – increased stress, anxiety, and self-reported symptoms of psychological distress.

Life throws curveballs. Deadlines loom, responsibilities pile up, and sometimes it feels like stress is your constant companion. But while a little stress is normal, chronic stress can wreak havoc on your mental well-being. It can zap your mood, drain your energy, and even lead to anxiety and depression. But wait, there's a bright light at the end of the tunnel! Your mental health plays a critical role in achieving your goals. When you're feeling down or overwhelmed, the motivation to take action can vanish faster than a free slice of pizza at a party. Imagine depression whispering doubts in your ear, making you question your ability to succeed. Or anxiety rearing its ugly head, convincing you to avoid setting goals altogether for fear of failure. Not exactly a recipe for reaching your full potential, is it?

Your mindset is where the magic happens. Your belief systems are like the internal GPS guiding your thoughts and actions. Understanding where these beliefs come from and how they impact your life is key.

Research has revealed a fascinating link between mindset and mental health. Studies show that young people with a fixed mindset (believing their talents and abilities are set in stone) were significantly more likely to experience anxiety and depression compared to those with a growth mindset (believing they can learn and improve through effort).

The good news? You, too, can cultivate a growth mindset! Think of your brain as a jungle gym – always growing and forming new connections. You can build powerful neural pathways that support a growth mindset by embracing new experiences, challenging yourself, and learning from setbacks.

Imagine yourself encountering a roadblock on your journey towards achieving a goal. With a fixed mindset, you might see it as a permanent obstacle, a sign you're not good enough. But with a growth mindset, you see it as a temporary hurdle, a chance to learn and grow. You dust yourself off, develop a new strategy, and keep moving forward. Powerful, right? Dr. Jacob Towery, a psychology expert, puts it perfectly: *"The exciting news about mindsets is that they are absolutely changeable."* Cognitive therapy is built on the idea that you can challenge negative thoughts and limiting beliefs. You have the power to rewrite your internal script and choose a growth mindset that empowers you to achieve your goals and live a fulfilling life. Life throws challenges; sometimes, those challenges can knock the wind out of your sails. Hitting a motivational slump is normal. But there are simple strategies you can incorporate into your routine to reignite your motivation and keep moving forward.

Challenge Negative Thinking

We all have that inner voice that loves to point out setbacks. Instead of dwelling on what went wrong, reframe the situation. Focus on your strengths and accomplishments. Did you experience a setback? Great! That's valuable learning that helps you improve.

Build Your Support System

Don't do it alone! Lean on your friends, family, or even a therapist. Having a reliable support system provides a wellspring of encouragement and keeps you accountable. They're your personal hype team, cheering you on every step of the way.

Make Goals Manageable

In case you're feeling overwhelmed by a giant goal, chop it into bite-sized chunks. Taking small, achievable steps makes even the most ambitious dreams feel manageable. This allows you to celebrate mini-victories along the way, which keeps motivation high.

Prioritize Self-Care

It's not selfish, it's essential. Getting enough sleep, eating healthy foods, and engaging in activities you enjoy all contribute to your mental well-being. When you take care of yourself, you're fueling your motivation engine for long-term success.

Remember, a growth mindset is key. Believe in your ability to learn and grow, and watch your goals transform from dreams to reality!

Embracing Growth

'"...as you begin to understand the fixed and growth mindsets, you will see exactly how one thing leads to another - how a belief that your qualities are carved in stone leads to a host of thoughts and actions, and how a belief that your qualities can be cultivated leads to a host of different thoughts and actions, taking you down an entirely different road.'" – Carol Dweck, Ph.D., Stanford Researcher and Professor

Ready to ditch the "fixed mindset" and step into a world of possibilities now?

A growth mindset isn't just about achieving goals; it's about embracing the journey of continuous learning and development. Think of it this way: by acknowledging past tendencies as stepping stones, not limitations, you open yourself up to future growth. Here's how you can reframe some common fixed beliefs:

Fixed Mindset: Perseverance and trying hard are the best ways to develop and expand one's capabilities. (This implies that effort is the only ingredient, and reaching a certain level may be impossible.)

Growth Mindset: Perseverance and trying hard *is* crucial for development, but so are learning new strategies and seeking out challenges that push your boundaries. Every obstacle you overcome expands your capabilities.

A growth mindset isn't just for specific skills. It applies to everything!

From Envy to Empowered Learning:

- **Fixed Mindset:** They are great at this. I'll never be like them. (This breeds envy and resignation.)

- **Growth Mindset:** Wow, they're fantastic! What techniques can I learn from them to thrive in my own skill set? Maybe I can observe their approach, ask them for advice, or find resources to develop similar skills. Their success inspires me to grow!

From Self-Doubt to Self-Improvement:

- **Fixed Mindset Belief:** I'm not good at this. (This label discourages effort.)

- **Growth Mindset Reframe:** I will train myself to improve at this. There might be more challenging aspects, but with dedication and practice, I can improve. Let's find learning resources, practice regularly, and track my progress!

From Negative Labels to Owning Your Progress:

- **Fixed Mindset Belief:** I'm terrible at time management. (This creates a sense of helplessness.)

- **Growth Mindset Reframe:** Time management has been challenging for me. This acknowledges the issue without resorting to negative labels. Now, I can create a plan. Maybe I need to schedule tasks more realistically, set reminders, or explore time management techniques.

As you embark on this exciting journey, don't be afraid to try new things! Experimentation is how you discover hidden talents and uncover new possibilities. Take a class, join a group, or try a different approach.

View challenges and setbacks as failures and opportunities to learn and grow. Every mistake holds a valuable lesson. Reflect on what went wrong, adjust your approach, and keep moving forward.

A healthy mind fuels a growth mindset! Take care of yourself by getting enough sleep, managing stress in healthy ways, and engaging in activities you enjoy. A balanced and positive mental state is essential for fostering a growth mindset.

Remember, growth is a continuous process. By consistently practicing these strategies and embracing the power of growth beliefs, you'll be well on your way to achieving your goals and reaching your full potential.

Chapter 3: Imperfectly Perfect

Imagine walking into a room full of flawless people, like airbrushed versions of themselves. Every laugh is perfect, every outfit impeccably coordinated, every answer brimming with brilliance.

Now, imagine the pressure. You feel every misplaced hair, every awkward silence, every forgotten fact like a glaring neon sign screaming "IMPERFECT!"

According to the Merriam-Webster dictionary, perfectionism is defined as "a disposition to regard anything short of perfection as unacceptable."[8] Breaking it down word by word, "disposition" refers to a general tendency or habitual attitude. So, perfectionism is a way of thinking where anything less than flawless is seen as simply not good enough.[9]

Envision the weight of that definition. It implies that if you're not perfect, you're somehow unacceptable.

That is the life of a perfectionist.

It's a constant battle against a standard that doesn't exist, a recipe for anxiety and self-loathing.

Now, picture the world holding this belief that perfection is the only possible way to exist. From this perspective, the world isn't just rejecting you as you are, but you're also rejecting yourself for who you are. But guess what? You were never meant to be perfect. The dictionary definition? Forget it. Let's rewrite

---

[8] https://springhill.cc/sermons/daniel-a-spirit-of-excellence-1/
[9] https://bellevuechristiancounseling.com/articles/never-good-enough-battling-perfectionism-part-i-of-ii

the story. **Perfectionism** isn't about striving for excellence; it's about demanding flawlessness for yourself and others. The American Psychological Association chimes in with another definition: "the tendency to demand of others or of oneself an extremely high or even flawless level of performance, more than what is required by the situation." This definition highlights how perfectionism isn't just about yourself. It can also be about the expectations you place on others.

It emphasizes the unrealistic standards that perfectionists set, often exceeding what's necessary.

Perfection is a myth.

Everyone, and I mean EVERYONE, has flaws. That dimple on your cheek you might consider a blemish? It's what makes you smile unique. That time, you tripped in front of your crush? Hilarious story material now, right?

Our imperfections are the brushstrokes that paint the beautiful portrait of who we are. They're not mistakes to be hidden but experiences that shape us. They're the lessons learned, the battles fought, the journeys that make us who we are today.

ThePower of Imperfections

Have you ever felt like you're constantly playing catch-up with some imaginary perfect version of yourself? Perfectionism is a sneaky villain that can steal our joy and hold us back from reaching our full potential. But what if I told you that your imperfections are actually your superpowers in disguise? It's easy to feel defined by our strengths, the areas where we naturally excel. But what about the skills we haven't quite mastered? We all have these so-called "**weaknesses**" – areas where we don't naturally shine. Maybe you're a whiz at planning and organization, but last-minute changes send you scrambling. Or perhaps public speaking makes your palms sweat and your voice squeak. These weaknesses aren't barricades but detours on the path to self-discovery.

Embracing this "weakness" could be a chance to challenge ourselves to learn the art of going with the flow. It might be scary at first, but conquering that fear and developing a new skill are wins for your personal growth.

You can transform fear into a powerful motivator by turning what once felt like a weakness into a strength.

Similarly, the fluttering in your chest and the clammy palms –are the physical manifestations of **performance anxiety**.

That knot in your stomach before a big presentation or stage performance? Totally normal.

According to the American Psychological Association, performance anxiety is "extreme nervousness experienced before or during participation in an activity taking place in front of an audience." The problem is we often focus so much on being perfect that we miss the joy of sharing our talents.

Imagine a comedian bombing a joke. The perfectionist might see the entire performance as a failure. But what about the other jokes that landed? A more self-accepting approach focuses on the strengths – the laughs, the connection with the audience. Remember, the courage to get up there and perform is a feat in itself. Surveys show that nearly 75% of people have a fear of public speaking.[10] Knowing this commonality can be a confidence booster. If you do stumble, it's okay! Most people won't even notice. Focus on letting your charisma shine through, and the audience will root for you.

Your imperfections are what make you……*you*. They tell the story of your experiences and the challenges you have overcome, adding depth and authenticity to your personality.

Think of your favorite celebrities, musicians, or artists. Do they have zero flaws? Probably not! But their flaws don't define them – they make them relatable, interesting, and human.

Embracing your imperfections isn't about giving up on growth. It's about celebrating your journey, flaws, and all. It's about recognizing the beauty in the messy, the quirky, the wonderfully imperfect you.

Owning Your Imperfections

Remember that sinking feeling you get scrolling through social media, bombarded with impossibly perfect profiles? It's easy to feel like your "flaws" – your height, your laugh, your tendency to overthink everything – somehow hold you back. But the thing is that those "flaws" are actually the secret weapon to unlock a life brimming with confidence and fulfillment.

Let's take physical imperfections first. Maybe you're vertically challenged in a world obsessed with height. Society might shove these unrealistic beauty standards down your

---

[10] https://www.supportivecareaba.com/statistics/fear-of-public-speaking-statistics#:~:text=According%20to%20the%20National%20Institute,their%20fear%20of%20public%20speaking.

throat, but it's all a carefully crafted illusion. Think of iconic stars like Danny DeVito or Kristen Bell – their talent and charisma light up the room, regardless of height.

These societal expectations are like a bad case of the hiccups – annoying and distracting, but ultimately not a reflection of your worth. We're bombarded with these images from a young age, making us question our own awesomeness based on some arbitrary ruler. But guess what? You can rewrite the script!

Instead of feeling less-than because you're not a walking billboard, focus on what makes you you. Maybe your shorter stature makes you a whiz at navigating crowded spaces or a master of killer dance moves (think Shakira!). Remember, confidence and self-acceptance are the ultimate power moves, no matter your height on the measuring stick.

Now, let's dive into the emotional and behavioral "flaws" that might make you say, *"Ugh, that's so me!"* But what if we flipped the script on those, too?

This isn't just some feel-good rhetoric. It's about reshaping how you view yourself. Imagine looking in the mirror and seeing not a list of faults but a collection of unique traits that add up to something wonderful. It's a powerful shift in perspective, and it starts with a little exercise.

Activity 1: The Flip Side Chart

Grab a piece of paper and make two columns. In the first column, list what you perceive as your weaknesses. Be honest— this is for your eyes only. In the second column, write down the flip side of those Weaknesses, The Hidden Strengths.

Weakness	Flip Side
Indecisive	Open-Minded
Procrastinator	Works Well Under Pressure
Sensitive	Compassionate Towards Others

See what we did there? It's all about perspective. Your perceived flaws are just another facet of your strengths.

Activity 2: Self-Reflection Chart

Now, let's take it a step further. Create a chart with four columns: strengths, weaknesses, things to improve on, and things to accept.

Strengths	Weaknesses	Things to Improve On	Things to Accept
Empathy	Overthinking	Time management	Height
Creativity	Self-doubt	Public speaking skills	Freckles
Determination	Impatience	Delegation	Past mistakes

Fill this out honestly. You'll start to see a more balanced picture of yourself. You have undeniable strengths, areas where you can grow, and traits that you need to accept as part of who you are.

By doing these exercises, you remind yourself daily that perfection is a fable. What's real is your ability to embrace every part of yourself, celebrate your strengths, and acknowledge your areas for growth without beating yourself up. Self-acceptance is a powerful antidote to the societal pressures and unrealistic standards we face every day. You will wake up every morning and feel at peace with who you are. I would not worry about whether you measure up to some arbitrary standard, but I know deep down that you are enough. This doesn't mean you stop striving to improve—it means you recognize that you are a work in progress, and that's perfectly okay.Accepting yourself fully is like giving yourself a huge, comforting hug. It's saying, "I am who I am, with all my quirks and qualities, and that's more than enough." It's about investing in your growth while loving who you are.

Embrace it. Celebrate it because the world doesn't need another cookie-cutter version of perfection. It needs you— authentic, imperfect, and utterly extraordinary.

Negative Bias

You might ask yourself, *"Why is embracing our differences so darn hard?"* Well, It all boils down to a sneaky little brain quirk called **negative bias.**

It's like a built-in negativity filter.

Remember those embarrassing childhood moments that still make you cringe? Negative bias makes us cling to those memories more readily than the times we totally rocked it. We tend to focus on the negative comment from a stranger rather than the compliment a friend gave. It's like negativity gets VIP treatment in our brains. This tendency makes us more likely to register negative stimuli over positive ones, also known as positive-negative asymmetry. It's a psychological phenomenon that explains why we notice, think about, remember, and respond to negativity more readily than positivity. Imagine a scenario: you're at a social gathering, and someone makes a passing comment about your appearance. Even if it's one comment amid dozens of compliments, it sticks with you like a thorn. Why is that? Humans often:

1. Retain traumatic experiences more easily,

2. Remember negative comments more clearly than positive ones,

3. React more intensely to negative stimuli,

4. Ruminate on negative thoughts more frequently than positive ones.

By focusing intently on what we see as our weaknesses, we spotlight them and let them overshadow our positive attributes.

This negativity bias starts young. Studies show that babies are initially drawn to positive stimuli, like happy voices and smiling faces. But as they grow, something shifts. Their brains become more sensitive to negativity. It's like a survival mechanism — negativity helps us avoid danger. However, this can backfire in adulthood. We hold ourselves back and limit our potential by constantly magnifying our perceived flaws.

Picture yourself standing in front of a giant spotlight. Everything you focus on gets bathed in that bright light. So, if you're constantly fixated on your weaknesses, guess what gets magnified? Yep, those very flaws start to define your self-perception. Negative bias doesn't stop with self-perception. It also impacts how we make decisions. Remember that time you chickened out of asking for a raise because you focused on the slim possibility of rejection instead of the potential for a bigger paycheck?

Yup, negative bias is at play.

Nobel Prize-winning researchers Daniel Kahneman and Amos Tversky found that people tend to place more weight on negative aspects than positive ones when making decisions.[11] We tend to weigh negative outcomes much more heavily than positive ones. Losing $20 feels way worse than finding $20, even though they cost the same amount.

This negativity bias can also wreak havoc on our mental health. When we dwell on negative thoughts and struggle to find the good in situations, it can lead to anxiety and depression.

Isn't it fascinating how our minds seem to cling to negative thoughts like magnets? You make one tiny mistake, and suddenly, it feels like the end of the world.

But Wait, There's Hope!

You can shift your focus from negativity to positivity and embrace the unique person you are.

1. Halt Negative Thoughts in Their Tracks

Replaying a past mistake in your mind, over and over. It's draining, isn't it? The next time this happens, try this simple yet powerful technique: stop, take a deep breath, and shift your focus. Instead of pondering over the mistake, consider what that

---

[11] https://thedecisionlab.com/reference-guide/economics/prospect-theory

experience taught you. How has it shaped you? Perhaps it made you more resilient or highlighted a strength you didn't know you had.

For instance, if you're berating yourself for a presentation that didn't go as planned, remind yourself of the courage it took to stand up there in the first place. Reflect on the feedback you received and how it can help you improve next time. This shift in perspective transforms a negative experience into a valuable learning opportunity.

2. Reframe Your Perceptions

Life is full of ups and downs, but how you interpret these events makes all the difference. Instead of seeing a challenge as a setback, try to view it as a stepping stone. Reframing doesn't mean ignoring potential dangers or serious incidents—it means balancing your view to include the positives.

Let's say you had a tough day at work. Think about what went wrong instead of focusing solely on what went right. Did you solve a problem? Help a colleague? Achieve a small goal? You create a more balanced and hopeful outlook by giving fair weight to the positive aspects.

3. Engage in Uplifting Activities

When negativity strikes, it's time to take action. Engaging in activities that bring you joy can help you break free from a negative mindset. It's about making a conscious effort to redirect your attention. If you've made a mistake, do something that lifts your spirits instead of spiraling into self-criticism. Go for a walk in nature, immerse yourself in a hobby, or call a friend who always knows how to make you laugh. These activities distract you from negative thoughts and reinforce positive emotions.

For example, if you love painting, lose yourself in your art for an hour. The act of creating something beautiful can be incredibly therapeutic and uplifting. It's a reminder that there's more to life than your mistakes—that you have talents and passions that define you.

4.Amplify Positive Experiences

Positive experiences require more effort to be remembered. Our brains are wired to transfer negative events into long-term memory quickly, but positive moments often need a bit more attention to stick. This is why it's crucial to savor and amplify the good times.

Start by keeping a journal where you jot down positive experiences and achievements. Reflect on these entries regularly to reinforce the positive memories. When something good happens, could you truly take a moment to savor it? Relive the emotions, describe the details, and let the happiness sink in.

For instance, if you receive a compliment at work, don't just brush it off. Take a moment to appreciate it. Write it down and revisit it when you need a boost. By consciously focusing on the positive, you train your brain to store these moments in your long-term memory, creating a more balanced and optimistic outlook.

The Despair of Comparison

Constantly comparing ourselves to others can be a fast track to feeling inadequate. You see someone's success and immediately think about your own perceived failures. You fixate on their strengths while downplaying or ignoring your own. This comparison game is unfair to you and based on incomplete information.

You see their highlight reel but not the behind-the-scenes struggles.

Looking at a successful entrepreneur, you always feel like you'll never measure up. But you might not see the sleepless nights, the failed attempts, and the personal sacrifices they made to get where they are. Everyone has their journey, and it's rarely as smooth as it appears from the outside.

So, how do we let go of this need to be perfect? It starts with the understanding that striving for perfection is unrealistic and detrimental to our well-being. By acknowledging that everyone has imperfections, we can begin to let go of the pressure to meet these impossible standards. This shift in mindset allows us to focus on being our authentic selves.

By embracing this mindset, we open the door to a powerful tool for personal growth: **self-compassion**.

Self-compassion is about being kind to ourselves when we fail or make mistakes. It involves three key components:

1. **Self-Kindness**: Treating yourself with the same care and understanding you would offer a friend. When you mess up, try speaking to yourself with kindness instead of

beating yourself up. Say, "It's okay, everyone makes mistakes. What can I learn from this?"

2. **Common Humanity**: Recognizing that everyone makes mistakes and that it's part of the human experience. You're not alone in your struggles. This realization can bring a sense of connection and reduce feelings of isolation.

3. **Mindfulness**: Observing your thoughts and feelings without judgment. Instead of getting caught up in negative emotions, take a step back and acknowledge them. This balanced perspective helps you avoid over-identifying with your flaws and failures.

Acceptance is at the core of self-compassion. It's about acknowledging your shortcomings, imperfections, and negative experiences as part of who you are. Studies have shown that people who approach past regrets with self-compassion rather than self-criticism experience greater personal improvement. By accepting these experiences, they're able to learn and grow from them.

Self-compassion also involves recognizing that flaws and imperfections are part of the shared human experience. This understanding can help us accept our own imperfections and those of others.

When we see our struggles mirrored in the lives of those around us, we feel empathy and connection. We're all in this together, doing the best we can with what we have.

Follow these practical steps to cultivate self-compassion in yourself:

1. **Practice Self-Kindness**: When you catch yourself being self-critical, pause and reframe your thoughts. Speak to yourself as you would to a dear friend.

2. **Embrace Imperfections**: List your perceived flaws and consider how they contribute to who you are. Celebrate these imperfections as part of your unique identity.

3. **Mindfulness Meditation**: Spend a few minutes each day in mindfulness meditation. Focus on your breath and observe your thoughts without judgment. This practice can help you develop a more balanced perspective on your experiences.

4. **Gratitude Journaling**: Write down things you're grateful for each day in a journal. This helps you shift your focus from what's wrong in your life to what's right.

5. **Connect with Others**: Share your experiences with friends or a support group. Hearing others' stories can remind you that you're not alone in your struggles.

6. **Set Realistic Goals**: Instead of aiming for perfection, set achievable goals that allow for growth and learning. Celebrate your progress, no matter how small.

Living Perfectly Imperfect

Our minds are wired for negativity bias that amplifies our flaws and dims our strengths. We hold onto embarrassing moments like a security blanket, replaying them on a loop long after their expiration date. We compare ourselves to the curated highlight reels on social media, feeling utterly inadequate in the face of those seemingly perfect lives. However, the secret most motivational posters forget to mention is that those "imperfections" are the magic ingredients to a truly fulfilling life. They're the lessons learned, the stumbles that made you stronger, the quirks that make you uniquely you.

Imagine a world where everyone strives for homogenous perfection. As the Chinese proverb goes, *"A journey of a thousand miles begins with a single step,"* but in this world, everyone would be stuck at step one, paralyzed by the fear of imperfection.

It would be a sterile, joyless place devoid of the vibrant sphere of human experience. It's the imperfections, the unexpected turns, the quirky detours that make our journeys so beautiful.

As you embark on the journey of living imperfectly, remember that it's a continuous process. There will be days when you struggle to be kind to yourself, and that's okay. What matters is that you keep trying. By embracing your imperfections, you're improving your relationship with yourself and creating a more compassionate world.

So, let go of the need to be perfect. Embrace your unique qualities, learn from your experiences, and celebrate the positive aspects of your life. Show up for yourself with grace and compassion.

You are worthy just as you are, and the world needs your authentic self. Again, you are worthy just as you are, and the world needs your authentic self. **Remember, the most beautiful stories are written on the pages of perfectly imperfect lives. Start writing yours today.**

Chapter 4: Relentless Compassion

Perfection isn't the goal—progress is.

We all stumble. We miss deadlines, say the wrong thing, or trip spectacularly in public. *Embarrassing, I know!*

But what separates those who bounce back from those who get stuck in a negativity loop is this beautiful thing called **self-compassion**.

Imagine self-compassion as a highway. On one side, there's the dark, winding road of self-criticism. It's a lonely place filled with judgment and blame. On the other side, there's the bright, open highway of self-compassion. This is where kindness and understanding are your constant companions, leading you towards growth and resilience.

The idea of self-compassion has deep roots in Eastern philosophy. Buddhism has long emphasized the importance of compassion—not just for others but for oneself. The teachings of the Buddha highlight the practice of **"Metta,"** or loving-kindness, which is extended to all beings, including oneself.

Buddhist monks have practiced self-compassion through meditation and mindfulness for thousands of years. They believe that cultivating compassion within can radiate kindness to the world. This ancient practice is not just about being nice; it's a philosophical way to achieve inner peace and enlightenment.

Fast forward to the Western world. Historically, Western philosophy has often emphasized self-discipline and criticism as paths to improvement. Think of the stoic philosophers who valued resilience and toughness, sometimes at the expense of self-kindness. However, as psychology evolved as a field, thinkers began to explore the idea of self-compassion more deeply. The humanistic psychology movement, with pioneers like Carl Rogers and Abraham Maslow, shifted the focus towards self-acceptance and unconditional positive regard. They believed that treating oneself with kindness was essential for personal growth and self-actualization.

Religious teachings across cultures have also touched upon the idea of self-compassion. In Christianity, the concept of ***"love thy neighbor as thyself"*** implies that self-love is foundational to loving others. This perspective encourages believers to extend forgiveness and kindness inwardly as well as outwardly.

Similarly, in Hinduism, the practice of **"Ahimsa,"** or non-violence, emphasizes the idea that you should not harm yourself through harsh judgment or self-criticism. Instead, treat yourself with the same respect and gentleness you offer others.

Over time, these ideas evolved. Self-compassion has now become a hot topic in psychological research, thanks in large part to the work of Dr. Kristin Neff. Her groundbreaking studies and development of the **Self-Compassion Scale** have brought scientific rigor to the ancient wisdom of self-kindness.

Dr. Neff's research has shown that self-compassion is not only beneficial but essential for mental health and well-being. Studies have shown that self-compassion fosters a positive body image, helping you appreciate yourself for who you are, imperfections and all.[12] It equips you to handle life's inevitable

---

[12] https://www.ncbi.nlm.nih.gov/pmc/articles/PMC10669661/

ebbs and flows with grace and strength, acting as a personal toolbox for effective coping. When faced with failure, self-compassion doesn't let you wallow. Instead, it helps you pick yourself up, dust yourself off, learn from your mistakes, and keep moving forward with renewed determination.

It even helps you manage stress, keeping those pesky fight-or-flight responses at bay and allowing you to stay calm and focused.

Think of being compassionate as putting yourself in someone else's shoes, feeling their pain, and wanting to help. Now, turn that empathy inward.

There are three core components to self-compassion: mindfulness, common humanity, and kindness. These elements are distinct but interact as a system, and all three must be present in a self-compassionate mindset to make it healthy and stable.

1. Self-Kindness vs. Judgement

Imagine how you would treat a close friend who's going through a tough time. You would probably offer them words of encouragement, a shoulder to cry on, or maybe just a listening ear. That's exactly how you need to treat yourself.

When you stumble or fall short—and you will, because you're human—take the highway to self-compassion. Don't let those negative emotions hijack your mind and send you into a tailspin. Instead, give yourself a break. Recognize that it's okay to make mistakes and that these moments are opportunities for growth, not reasons for self-flagellation. If unexpected bills arrive or a project falls flat at work, the old you might resort to harsh self-criticism – the *"you should have known better"* kind of talk. But defensive reactions or harsh self-criticism won't get you anywhere.

In fact, they can stymie your development and keep you stuck in a negative loop.

Instead, respond with self-compassion. Acknowledge that setbacks are part of life and offer yourself some understanding. *"Hey, this is tough, but everyone makes mistakes. What can I learn from this, and how can I move forward?"* This shift in perspective can lead to thoughtful changes in how you handle life's challenges.

As Dr. Kristin Neff puts it perfectly, *"At the most basic level, self-compassion simply requires being a good friend to ourselves."* Isn't that a beautiful sentiment? Wouldn't you rather have a supportive friend by your side than a constant critic?

2. Common Humanity vs. Isolation

It's easy to fall into the trap of thinking you're the only one struggling, leading to feelings of loneliness and shame. This sense of isolation can lead to irrational thoughts, convincing us that our pain is unique and separating us from others.

However, this couldn't be further from the truth.

Remember that you're not alone when you hit a bump in the road. Your experiences, challenges, and failures are part of the shared human experience. By recognizing this, you can foster a sense of connection and belonging. We're all imperfectly perfect in our own ways, and that's what makes us beautifully human. By activating our common humanity, we acknowledge that our struggles connect us to others rather than separate us. We recognize that countless others have faced similar difficulties and perhaps even triumphed over them. This realization fosters a sense of connection and belonging. It reminds us that we're not alone in our struggles and that there's strength in shared experience.

Think of a time you felt compassion for someone else's mistake or experience. Can you extend the same understanding to yourself when faced with personal challenges?

3. Mindfulness vs. Over-Identification

The third pillar of self-compassion is mindfulness, contrasted with over-identification. Mindfulness involves taking a balanced, non-reactive approach to our experiences, especially our suffering.

It's about observing our thoughts and feelings without getting swept away by them or trying to suppress them. This mindful approach allows us to accept the present moment as it is, with all its imperfections and challenges.

On the other hand, over-identification is when we become so entangled with the negative emotions that they define us. We exaggerate our difficulties and let them take over our sense of self. Mindfulness helps us avoid this trap by encouraging us to turn towards our pain with curiosity and openness.

Instead of becoming overwhelmed by difficult thoughts and feelings, we acknowledge them and let them pass through us like clouds drifting across the sky. This balanced approach prevents us from becoming overly identified with our suffering and allows us to maintain a clearer, more compassionate perspective. It's crucial not to suppress or ignore your negative feelings, but don't let them run the show. Acknowledge them, understand them, and then gently steer yourself back to a place of balance.

Imagine you're a captain navigating a ship through a storm. You wouldn't ignore the storm but wouldn't let it sink your ship, either. Instead, you'd adjust your sails and keep moving forward. That's how you should handle your negative emotions—acknowledge them, but don't be ruled by them.

Dr. Kristin Neff's self-compassion scale can be used to assess a person's natural levels of self-compassion scale. This scale helps measure self-compassion and correlate scores with various positive outcomes.

Self-compassionate people are more likely to have a grounded and continuous sense of self-worth, independent of societal standards and expectations.

They display higher levels of emotional intelligence, meaning they're better at recognizing, understanding, and managing their own emotions. This emotional intelligence fosters healthier relationships and greater personal satisfaction.

Moreover, self-compassionate individuals are ambitious about learning and personal growth.

They're more willing to take risks and face new challenges because they don't fear failure. Instead of developing imposter syndrome, they approach new opportunities with curiosity and resilience. They show contentment and optimism about their lives, maintaining hope and a positive outlook even in the face of adversity. In contrast, those who lack self-compassion are more likely to base their self-worth on external validation and societal expectations. They might experience a disconnect with their emotions, finding it difficult to accept and understand their feelings.

This emotional disconnect can lead to unhealthy coping mechanisms, such as substance abuse, to numb their pain.

Self-compassionate people are also better equipped to cope with personal and professional challenges. They face difficulties head-on with a sense of balance and calm, using healthy strategies to manage stress. On the flip side, those without self-compassion might turn to unhealthy coping methods like alcohol and drug abuse as they struggle to handle life's pressures.

Embracing Self-Compassion in Daily Life

Self-compassion isn't a switch you flip for instant happiness. It's a practice, a commitment to treating yourself with the same kindness and understanding you'd offer a loved one. While it aims to alleviate suffering, it doesn't promise a world free of pain. Difficult emotions are inevitable, but self-compassion equips you to navigate them with grace.

The goal isn't to suppress or ignore your pain. It's to acknowledge it mindfully and then respond with self-care and kindness. Imagine a loved one going through a heartbreak. You wouldn't berate them, would you? You'd offer a hug, a listening ear, and words of comfort. This is the essence of self-compassion – extending that same warmth and support to yourself. By doing this, you foster self-love and connection. You create a safe space for growth and transformation, allowing the pain to transform you without breaking you. Here are some exercises to promote this powerful practice:

1. Treating Yourself as a Friend

Consider how you support a close friend going through a tough time. You offer them empathy, encouragement, and a non-judgmental presence. Now, imagine applying the same approach to yourself. Grab a sheet of paper and jot down what you would say and do for a friend in distress. Be specific about your words and actions.

Next, think about how you typically respond to yourself when facing similar troubles. Compare the two approaches and note any differences. This exercise highlights the contrast between your self-compassion and your self-criticism. Realize the positive changes that could occur if you treated yourself with the same kindness you extend to your friends.

Now, rewrite your internal script using the words you'd use for your friend. Speak with kindness and understanding. Remember, you deserve the same compassion you readily give to others.

2. Using Supportive Touch

Feeling overwhelmed? Supportive touch offers a simple yet powerful way to activate your body's calming mechanisms and provide a sense of safety. Initially, it might feel awkward, but your body will respond positively to the physical gesture of warmth. Research has shown that physical touch releases oxytocin, which fosters a sense of security, reduces cardiovascular stress, and enhances well-being.

Here's how to practice supportive touch:

- Begin by taking 2-3 deep breaths when you notice you're under stress.

- Gently place one or both hands over your heart, feeling the warmth and gentle pressure.

- If you like, make small circles with your hands.

- Focus on your chest as it rises and falls with each breath.

- Stay with this feeling until the stress dissipates.

Alternatively, you can cross your arms and give yourself a gentle squeeze, cradle your face in your hands, or cup one hand in the other and place it in your lap. These actions activate your body's care system, promoting calmness and self-compassion.

3. Modifying Critical Self-Talk

Start by becoming aware of your self-critical thoughts. This might be challenging since self-criticism often becomes an automatic habit. Reflect on what you say to yourself when you feel bad about something. Notice the words, tone of voice, and key phrases. Pay attention to whether this critical voice resembles someone from your past who was harsh towards you. The more you recognize this inner critic, the more you'll notice its presence.

Now, soften this inner voice with compassion. If your self-critic says something like, *"You're gross,"* in response to gaining weight, counter it with a compassionate perspective.

Acknowledge the concern but shift towards kindness: *"I know this is a setback, but being judgmental isn't helpful. Let's approach this with a compassionate mindset."*

Shift your perspective. Imagine a supportive friend offering their words. What would they say?

For example: *"I understand that gaining weight wasn't part of the plan. I want you to feel good in your body. Let's focus on how we can improve our habits and take note of any positive changes, like how our clothes fit. It could be muscle gain, not just weight."*

Remember, kindness is key. As you consistently challenge negativity with compassion, a more supportive inner voice will emerge

4. Keeping a Self-Compassion Journal

Journaling is an effective way to process emotions and experiences. Set aside a few quiet moments each day to reflect on the events that affected you negatively. Write down incidents that caused you pain, made you feel judged, or led to self-criticism. For each event, apply the core components of self-compassion: mindfulness, common humanity, and kindness.

Mindfulness involves acknowledging your feelings without judgment. Common humanity reminds you that suffering is a shared human experience. Kindness encourages you to respond to yourself with empathy and understanding.

For example, if you had a challenging day at work, write about how you felt and how you can be kind to yourself in that situation. Reflect on how others might face similar challenges and offer yourself the same compassion you would extend to them. We all know the feeling – you want to be kinder to yourself and treat yourself with love and understanding. But something always seems to get in the way. That voice in your head whispers doubts, societal pressures push you towards unrealistic goals, and maybe you even feel a tinge of guilt at the thought of "letting yourself off the hook."

Well, guess what? You're not alone! Self-compassion is a superpower, but unlocking it can feel like trying to crack a vault with a butter knife.

We live in a world obsessed with achievement and perfection. Everywhere we look, there are images of "perfect" lives, perfect bodies, perfect careers. It's enough to make anyone feel like they're constantly falling short. Realize that these are unrealistic standards and chasing them will only lead to frustration and self-doubt.

Define success and happiness on YOUR terms. Ditch the comparison game! What truly matters to you? Is it climbing the corporate ladder, traveling the world, or spending quality time with loved ones? Focus on your own values and set goals that align with them. Surround yourself with positive influences who celebrate you for who you are, not who society expects you to be. Remember, it's your life, your journey, and you get to decide what makes you happy.

Maybe the idea of self-compassion makes you squirm a little. Is it just a fancy way of being lazy or going easy on yourself? Absolutely not! Self-compassion is about acknowledging your struggles, accepting your imperfections, and offering yourself support and encouragement. It's not about coddling yourself or shirking responsibility. It's about self-care, and guess what? Taking care of yourself is essential for long-term success and happiness! If you wouldn't beat up a friend for making a mistake, why do it to yourself?

Sometimes, the biggest obstacle is not knowing that self-compassion is an option. Many of us were never taught to prioritize our own well-being, so that it can feel foreign or even uncomfortable.

But self-compassion is a skill anyone can learn! Read books on the topic, listen to podcasts, and take a workshop. The more you learn about its benefits, the easier it will be to embrace it.

Start small – acknowledge your efforts and celebrate your successes, no matter how big or small.

Forgive yourself for your mistakes and use them as opportunities to grow. With daily practice, self-compassion will become a natural part of your life, a superpower waiting to be unleashed!

So, there you have it, the transformative power of relentless compassion. In a world that often prioritizes achievement over self-care, it's easy to lose sight of the importance of being kind to ourselves. But as we've explored in this chapter, self-compassion isn't just a fluffy concept—it's a practical tool for navigating life's ups and downs with grace and resilience.

From the ancient wisdom to the cutting-edge research of modern psychology, the message is clear: treating ourselves with the same kindness and understanding we offer others is beneficial and essential for our well-being. Embrace the three pillars of self-compassion and watch as they become your guiding lights through life's challenges. So go ahead, befriend yourself. Offer a listening ear when you stumble, a comforting hug when you falter. And remember, in a world where you can be anything, choose to be relentlessly compassionate—to yourself and to others.

Chapter 5: Passion into Action

Have you ever felt that electric thrill, that deep yearning that pulls you towards something bigger than yourself?

That is the power of **passion**.

It's the fuel that gets you out of bed in the morning, the invisible force pushing you towards your goals. It's the reason you spend hours lost in an activity, a feeling so intense it defines who you are.

Passion isn't just a fleeting fancy; it's the compass that guides you to your purpose. It whispers about the things that truly matter, the activities that ignite a spark within you and make you feel alive. It's the reason you lose track of time painting, writing that novel, or volunteering for a cause close to your heart.

The beauty of passion lies in feeling it and **acting upon it**. Passion thrives on action, on turning that spark into a roaring fire.

When you engage in activities that ignite your soul, you experience a surge of positive emotions. It's like a shot of happiness directly into your brain!

Studies consistently show that channeling your passion leads to a more **sustainable psychological well-being**.[13] This means a life filled with joy, happiness, and a deep sense of satisfaction.

Imagine yourself thriving, not just surviving. Imagine feeling empowered, growing as a person, and achieving things you never thought possible. That's the power of putting your passion into

---

[13] https://psywb.springeropen.com/articles/10.1186/2211-1522-2-1

action. Passion isn't just a one-time burst of excitement—it's a sustained force that shapes our actions and attitudes over time. It plays a critical role in our psychological well-being, influencing how we experience life and how we grow as individuals.

Research has also shown that the benefits of pursuing your passions extend far beyond your mental well-being. We're talking about improved physical health, stronger relationships, and even higher levels of performance in your career or studies.

Sure, life will throw challenges your way, and there will be times when negativity creeps in. But when you cultivate your passions, you build a powerful defense system against setbacks. You create a buffer against dissatisfaction and stagnation.

Passion becomes your safety net, reminding you why you started on this journey in the first place.

Not All Passions Are Created Equal

We all have those things that set our souls on fire, activities that pull us in and make us lose track of time. But did you know there's a science to passion?

Psychologists have identified two distinct types of passion, and understanding the difference is key to harnessing this powerful force for good.

The **Dualistic Model of Passion (DMP)** sheds light on this fascinating concept. This theory proposes that passion exists on a spectrum with two distinct sides: harmonious and obsessive.

Harmonious Passion

Imagine a passion that fuels your creativity, propels you towards self-improvement, and leaves you feeling energized and fulfilled.

When you have harmonious passion, you engage in activities you love because you choose to, not because you feel compelled to. This type of passion is an **"autonomous internalization"**—it's self-driven and self-rewarding.

It arises from a genuine interest in an activity, a deep sense of enjoyment, and a strong belief in its importance.

Imagine you love painting. With harmonious passion, you paint because it brings you joy and fulfillment. You can balance your painting with other aspects of your life, maintaining a healthy equilibrium.

Harmonious passion also fosters **flexibility**. You have the freedom to choose when and how you participate in the activity, allowing you to adjust your schedule or intensity without feeling like you're failing.

So, if an activity becomes detrimental to your well-being, you can step away. Harmonious passion empowers you to prioritize your overall health and well-being, making adjustments as needed. Here's what sets harmonious passion apart:

- **Autonomy:** This passion stems from an internal drive, not external pressures. You choose to engage in this activity because it brings you joy and fulfills you.

- **Mastery:** Harmonious passion thrives on a healthy challenge. It's the desire to learn, grow, and constantly improve your skills in this domain.

- **Balance:** This type of passion doesn't consume your entire life. It coexists harmoniously with other aspects of your well-being, like relationships and career.

The benefits of harmonious passion are undeniable. Studies show that it leads to:

- **Increased well-being:** Engaging in activities you love boosts happiness, life satisfaction, and overall mental health.

- **Enhanced skills:** Harmonious passion fuels perseverance and a growth mindset, leading to improved skills and mastery in your chosen field.

- **Stronger relationships:** When you're fulfilled and energized, it spills over into your interactions with others, fostering stronger connections.

Obsessive Passion

Now, let's flip the coin and examine the other side of the spectrum – obsessive passion. This type of passion, while initially motivating, can become all-consuming and ultimately detrimental.

It breeds **rigidity**. The urge to participate becomes an unyielding force, making it difficult to adapt to changing circumstances. This can lead to:

- **Self-closure:** Obsessive passion can create a tunnel vision effect, causing you to neglect other important aspects of life like relationships, work, or self-care.

- **Missed opportunities:** Being fixated on one activity can prevent you from exploring new interests or experiences that might be enriching and fulfilling.

For example, a person with an obsessive passion for a sport might push themselves to the point of injury, ignoring the signals their body is sending them to rest. This can lead to long-term damage and a decrease in their overall quality of life.

Similarly, if you're obsessively passionate about your job, you might find yourself working long hours, neglecting your health, relationships, and other responsibilities.

Here's what defines obsessive passion:

- **External Pressures:** This passion stems from a desire for external validation, fear of failure, or a need to prove oneself to others.

- **Control:** Obsessive passion often manifests as a need for complete control over the activity and its outcomes. The fear of failure can be paralyzing.

- **Impaired Balance:** This passion can take over your life, leading to neglect of other important areas like health, relationships, or responsibilities.

While obsessive passion can initially provide a burst of motivation, the long-term consequences can be damaging:

- **Burnout:** The constant pressure and fear of failure associated with obsessive passion can lead to exhaustion and a feeling of emptiness.

- **Anxiety and Stress:** The need for control and fear of messing up can trigger chronic anxiety and stress, negatively impacting your well-being.

- **Neglect of Other Areas:** When one passion consumes you, other important aspects of life can suffer. Relationships can crumble, and responsibilities can fall by the wayside.

Obsessive passion is a double-edged sword; while it pushes you to excel, it can also be counterproductive, impairing your optimal functioning and well-being.

The **Self-Determination Theory (SDT)** sheds light on the connection between passion and our inherent drive for growth. SDT posits that humans are wired to explore and grow within our environment.

Through these experiences, we discover activities that spark our passions. These activities become deeply meaningful because they resonate with our core values and sense of self.

Over time, a few of these activities become our **passionate pursuits**. They're more than just hobbies; they become integral to who we are. This internalization can occur with both harmonious and obsessive passions. The key difference lies in how these passions impact our overall well-being. Research consistently shows that pursuing harmonious passions is a powerful tool for reducing stress and boosting happiness. A 2015 study by the University of California, Merced, and Penn State found that participants experienced a significant decrease in stress and sadness after engaging in activities they were passionate about.[14] Remember, lower stress levels translate to a more positive outlook on life and greater overall well-being.

Moreover, recent studies exploring the cultivation of passions among students have shown that learning about and developing passions can significantly enhance their excitement and engagement with their chosen subjects and college majors.

Mental health professionals also emphasize the importance of having a passion in a student's life, as it motivates them to learn, explore, and grow. This passion acts as a driving force, pushing students to achieve their goals and develop a deeper sense of purpose and satisfaction.

Striving for Harmony

The Dualistic Model of Passion helps us understand how passion affects our lives on a psychological level. Harmonious passion contributes to psychological well-being by promoting positive emotions, life satisfaction, and self-growth.

Conversely, obsessive passion can lead to psychological conflict and ill-being. The constant pressure to engage in the passion, even when it's detrimental, creates stress and dissatisfaction. But by understanding the two sides of passion and nurturing the harmonious kind, you can transform it into a powerful tool for growth, fulfillment, and a life fueled by genuine joy.

---

[14] https://panorama.ucmerced.edu/news/study-benefits-leisure-go-beyond-moment

- **Pursue Activities You Love:** Don't chase trends or societal expectations. Focus on activities that spark genuine joy and interest.

- **Embrace the Journey:** Focus on the process of learning, growth, and self-improvement, not just the end goal.

- **Maintain Balance:** Make sure your passion coexists with other important aspects of your life. Schedule time for self-care, relationships, and other responsibilities.

- **Celebrate Small Wins:** Acknowledge and celebrate your progress, no matter how small. This keeps you motivated and reinforces positive feelings.

Embrace the process, find your balance, and let your passion guide you towards a life well-lived.

So, how do you get started? The first step is to **uncover your passions**. But passion isn't always a loud, booming voice. Sometimes, it's a gentle whisper waiting to be heard. Here's how to tune in:

- **Reflect on what excites you:** What activities make you lose track of time? What topics spark your curiosity and ignite a sense of joy?

- **Explore your strengths:** What are you naturally good at? How can you leverage your skills to contribute to something meaningful?

- **Consider your values:** What matters most to you? Is it social justice, environmental protection, or fostering creativity in others?

Jot down everything that comes to mind. Don't worry about filtering or judging at this stage. The goal is to create a comprehensive list of your passions. Once you have a good starting point, look for common threads. Are there themes or underlying values that connect some of these passions?

By identifying these themes, you'll start to get a clearer picture of your **purpose**. Your purpose is your "why" – the deeper reason that drives you to make a difference. The guiding light illuminates your path and fuels your passion with a sense of meaning.

Now, let's bridge the gap between passion and action. Consider these strategies:

1. Start a Side Project

Transform your passion into a tangible project. Do you love crafting beautiful jewelry? Turn it into a part-time business selling your creations at local markets or online. The possibilities are endless!

These projects not only allow you to express your passion, but they can also have a surprising impact on your life. Even a small side hustle can generate additional income, boosting your financial security and freedom.

Running a side project also allows you to hone your skills in areas like marketing, finance, and communication. These skills can benefit both your professional and personal life.

Use your project as a platform to connect with others who share your passion. Build a community and foster a sense of belonging.

2. Networking and Continuous Learning

Your passion can open doors to numerous pathways, including opportunities for networking and continued growth. For instance, if you're passionate about community service, joining relevant organizations or associations can connect you with like-minded individuals who share your commitment to making a difference.

Connect with others who share your passion. Join local organizations, attend conferences, or find online communities. These connections offer invaluable support, mentorship, and opportunities for collaboration.

Fuel your passion by continuously learning and growing. Take workshops, read books on relevant topics, or watch online tutorials. The more you learn, the more you'll be able to contribute and make a real difference.

Additionally, seek guidance from experienced individuals in your field. Mentorship provides valuable insights and helps you navigate challenges. Fellowship with like-minded individuals fosters a sense of belonging and support.

3. Find Your Passion in Your Workplace

The daily grind. Does that phrase conjure images of endless emails, monotonous tasks, and a longing for something more? While your passion might not always reside within your specific job title, that doesn't mean it can't play a role in your work life. In fact, igniting your passion at work can lead to a more fulfilling and successful career. Let's face it: not every aspect of every job will be inherently exciting. But your passions – those activities that set your soul on fire — are vital to who you are. They represent the most creative, authentic aspects of yourself. Don't relegate them to the background! A recent study by Apollo Technical concluded that only 20% of employees in the US report feeling passionate about their jobs.[15] That translates to a staggering 80% who are disengaged and yearning for a deeper connection to their work. This disconnect affects not only individual well-being but also company culture and productivity.

Imagine the possibilities if those 80% could find a way to bridge the gap between their passions and their careers. The benefits are undeniable:

• **Increased Job Satisfaction:**

Finding a way to balance and create synchronicity between your passions and your career or business can help foster a better work environment.

When work aligns with your passions, it becomes more than just a paycheck. It becomes a source of fulfillment and purpose, leading to a more positive emotional state.

The average person spends up to one-third of their life working, so bringing passion into the workplace is beneficial for job satisfaction. In the modern workplace, both employees and employers strive to combine passion and work, making the job more enjoyable.

---

[15] https://zoetalentsolutions.com/employee-satisfaction-statistics/#:~:text=According%20to%20an%20article%20by,are%20truly%20passionate%20about%20them.

- **Enhanced Performance:**

Passion fuels motivation and dedication. Employees who are passionate about their work are more likely to go the extra mile, resulting in higher-quality output.

Bringing passion into your workplace is about more than just reaching long-term career goals. It's also about how you conduct your day-to-day life. Doing work you love can create a positive loop toward success. The trick is figuring out how to make yourself love your work. As your love for work gradually increases, it will naturally come to you. There may still be tasks you don't enjoy as much, but knowing the work is meaningful can make a big difference.

Additionally, as you become more confident in your skills and the projects you finish, you'll trust your instincts more and second-guess yourself less. Passion for something naturally leads to persistence, and this persistence will drive you to produce quality work, which leads to success. Passion and persistence go hand in hand, and as you align your work with your passion, everything from your environment to your personal life improves, fulfilling basic human psychological needs like belonging and self-actualization.

- **Improved Company Culture:**

A passionate workforce also creates a more positive and collaborative work environment. Employees who are invested in their work are more likely to be team players and brand ambassadors.

So, bring more passion into your workplace using these practical strategies:

1. **Shift Your Perspective:** Focus on the positive aspects of your work. Think about how your work improves the lives of others or builds products people need. By choosing to see the good in your work, you can start to feel more passionate about it.

2. **Connect with Others:** Become passionate about the people you work with. Develop close, harmonious relationships with your coworkers by getting to know them and their interests. Feeling like part of a team can enhance your work experience.

3. **Embrace Growth:** Look for opportunities within your workplace for personal and professional growth. Join clubs, participate in activities, or attend conferences. Stepping out of your comfort zone and working on new projects can feed your mind with new information and challenges.

4. **Take a Break:** Stepping away from work can help restore your passion for the workplace. Taking breaks can prevent burnout. Simple actions like leaving the office at a decent time, stepping away from your computer for ten minutes every few hours, not checking emails after business hours, or going for a walk during lunchtime can make a significant difference.

If, after trying these strategies, you still struggle to find passion in your work, it might be time for a reevaluation. Don't be afraid to address limiting beliefs or fear of failure holding you back. Consider exploring a career change that aligns more closely with your passions. This might not be an immediate solution, but it's a journey worth taking. Starting with self-awareness, taking consistent action, and believing in yourself can craft a career that ignites your passion and fuels your success. Remember, transformation takes time, so be patient with yourself.

Transforming passion into action is about more than just finding activities you enjoy; it's about integrating those passions into the very fabric of your life.

Remember, your passions are the sparks that ignite your enthusiasm and creativity. They are the compass guiding you towards your true potential. By embracing your passions and turning them into actionable pursuits, you enrich your life and inspire and uplift those around you.

This journey isn't always easy and may require persistence and self-discovery. However, the rewards of living passionately are immeasurable. Increased joy, deeper connections, and a sense of accomplishment are just a few of the benefits waiting for you.

So, take the first step today. Identify what excites you, explore ways to incorporate it into your daily life, and watch your passion transform into action. As you do, you'll find that the path to personal and professional fulfillment is paved with the vibrant energy of your passions, leading you to a life that meets your goals and nourishes your soul.

Transformation: Pathway to Purpose

Dr Amystique Church